HAYES PRESS

In the Beginning – Bible Studies in Genesis

Contents

1 CHAPTER ONE: INTRODUCTION (LAURIE BURROWS) 1

2 CHAPTER TWO: THE CREATION OF MAN (JOHN TERRELL) 8

3 CHAPTER THREE: THE FALL (GEORGE PRASHER JNR.) 15

4 CHAPTER FOUR: THE FLOOD (LINDSAY PRASHER) 23

5 CHAPTER FIVE: THE SCATTERING AT BABEL (TOM HYLAND) 29

6 CHAPTER SIX: THE CALL OF ABRAM (J.A. LENNOX BROWN) 35

7 CHAPTER SEVEN: ABRAHAM OFFERS UP ISAAC (GEORGE PRASHER SNR.) 40

8 CHAPTER EIGHT: JACOB AND ESAU (ALAN TOMS) 47

9 CHAPTER NINE: JACOB AND THE HOUSE OF GOD (R. LINDSAY) 54

10 CHAPTER TEN: JOSEPH AND HIS BROTHERS (JIM JOHNSTON) 61

11 CHAPTER ELEVEN: ISRAEL IN EGYPT (JOHN BAIRD) 68

12 CHAPTER TWELVE: CONCLUSION (LAURIE BURROWS) 75

ABOUT THE PUBLISHER 80

1

CHAPTER ONE: INTRODUCTION (LAURIE BURROWS)

In a day when the reliability of the Scriptures is widely questioned, it is salutary to examine the book of Genesis again. Accepted by faith, it provides a clear and authoritative account of creation, the origin of the human race, the entrance of sin into the human heart and God's dealings with men in the dawn of human history. In it are recorded divine judgements on wicked men and grace shown to the faithful, together with the oft-repeated promise of a Saviour who would provide the solution to the awful problem of sin, so that men might find divine favour and ultimate blessing.

The acknowledgement of these historical facts is fundamental to the correct appreciation of our position as God's creatures and members of a fallen race for whom God has provided a Saviour. But it is sad to reflect that most people find difficulty in taking the book of Genesis at its face value. Ordinary folk are being misled by men of superior intellectual ability who, lacking nevertheless the instruction of the Spirit of God, assert that the theory of evolution provides an adequate basis for the interpretation of scientific discoveries in a manner directly opposed to the Scriptures.

With supreme self-confidence they reject God's word and in its place they spin a flimsy web of human reasoning purporting to provide, without any acknowledgement of the Creator, details of the development of life and of the origin of the human race, matters about which no man can have knowledge apart from divine revelation. They advance purely mechanical explanations for the infinite variety and wonder of the universe, and pursue their argument to the logical conclusion that God has never been involved in this world's history. Man's successes and failures, the great religious and political movements and much else can be adequately explained, they say, in terms of man's environment and his innate tendencies, dismissing any possibility of divine intervention in human affairs.

Most people who have intellectual difficulties about the accuracy of a record of such antiquity or who question the truth of any events which appear to be beyond the range of present-day human experience are influenced by the sceptical attitude to the Scriptures which has developed over the last 200 years and can be traced to the almost universal acceptance of the theory of evolution. But not all who entertain the mechanical view of the universe are confessed atheists, in fact some would consider themselves to be Christians.

However, it is not generally realized that the denial of the divinely inspired accuracy of the book of Genesis involves rejection of the whole of the Bible, which is the basis of true belief in God and the source of all. genuine blessing to man. So that, religious leaders who embrace liberal views about the origin of man, undermine the very foundations of Christian belief and strangely enough seem to expect the structure to be strengthened in consequence! It is surely not overstating the case to say that today's violence, drug-taking, crime and lack of respect for authority are in the main attributable to this widespread maltreatment of God's word.

It is not difficult to show that the replacement in men's minds of the Creator by the theory of evolution as a complete explanation of origins not only impugns the book of Genesis but also is a denial of the truth of Scripture in its entirety. A simple study of a Bible with marginal references will demonstrate how closely interlocked every part of the Bible is. References to Genesis and quotations from it abound throughout both Old and New Testaments. For instance, creation as a direct act of the Creator is proclaimed in over 60 places in the books of Exodus, Nehemiah, Job, Psalms, Proverbs, Ecclesiastes, Isaiah, Jeremiah, Zechariah, Matthew, John, Acts, Romans, 1 Corinthians, Ephesians, Colossians, 1 Timothy, Hebrews, James, 2 Peter and Revelation.

Characters are mentioned and lessons are drawn by the Lord and the inspired writers of the New Testament in such a way as to leave no room for doubt that they accepted the historical accuracy of the Genesis record and were not drawing on a stock of Jewish folklore to teach New Testament doctrine. The name of Abraham occurs over one hundred times in the rest of Scripture, and his life and character permeate the whole of the sacred writings as the father of the faithful, the friend of God and the man whose spiritual vision penetrated the ages to see by faith the building of the eternal city (Hebrews 11:8-10). The unerring voice of the Master Himself confirms the existence of Abraham as a historical person (John 8:56-59), the creation of Adam and Eve (Matthew 19:4,5), the murder of Abel (Matthew 23:35), the guilt of Sodom (Luke 17:28-30) and the judgement of Lot's wife (Luke 17:32). Just as the infallible Teacher alludes in a significant manner to early events now disputed by modern theologians, so the apostle Paul, in his discourse on the certainty of the resurrection of the believer, confirms that Adam was the first man, contrasting him with Christ, the last Adam, in order to show that "as we have borne the image of the earthy, we shall also bear the image of the heavenly" (1 Corinthians 15:45-9).

Can the mention of Abel, Enoch, Noah, Abraham, Sarah, Isaac, Jacob, Esau and Joseph in Hebrews 11 be dismissed as references to ancient legends? This passage forms part of one of the deepest theological arguments in the whole of Scripture and such a suggestion is quite out of character with the tone of the letter to the Hebrews. Furthermore it is flatly contradicted in verse 40: "God having provided some better thing concerning us, that apart from us, they should not be made perfect". The faithful in this present age are thus irrevocably associated by divine decree with the godly of Genesis, the very existence of whom the critics think to deny.

If the inspired writer of the Hebrews considered the characters named in Genesis to be legendary it would have been out of the question for him to use them in this way to stress the fulfilment of blessing for the faithful of all ages. Scripture abounds with such instances of the confirmation of the literal trustworthiness of the book of Genesis, showing it to be an inseparable part of the Holy Scripture, having the same divinely inspired perfection.

Genesis knows nothing of the popular conception of a slow struggle by primitive man to overcome the difficulties of his environment and to develop the skills of civilisation. The Bible depicts Adam as a highly intelligent being, able to give names to all the animals (Genesis 2:20), which was no mean achievement. His grandson Enoch built a city (4:17). During the first millennium there were men who smelted brass and iron and forged them into implements, and there were others skilled in the use of musical instruments (4:21-22). No mention is made of cave-dwellers until the days of Abraham, when his nephew Lot left the city of Zoar in fear of the judgement of God to live in a cave with his two daughters (19:30). Another serious error widely held is that man at first worshipped many gods, but gradually acquired a truer knowledge of the one God. It is quite clear from Scripture that Adam, Eve, Cain and Abel had direct dealings with God, and in the days of Seth, son of Adam, men began to call upon the name of the Lord. Polytheism, like cave dwelling and savagery, was a later development arising from man's departure from God.

Genesis is therefore not the beginning of man's search after God, as some would have us believe, but the beginning of God's revelation of Himself to man. Although it is factually accurate, its purpose is not to teach history or any other branch of human knowledge but, as the introduction to God's written revelation, to impart spiritual instruction to the reader. It is sometimes called the seed-plot of the Bible because in it can be found in germinal form the main lines of spiritual teaching contained in the Scripture. Attention will be drawn to some of these as various contributors develop selected themes from this important book. It is our earnest prayer that this book will stimulate interest in what God has caused to be written in His Book for the people of today about creation and the early history of mankind. Although thousands of years have gone by, human nature has not changed, and the spiritual experiences of a man like Jacob can be shared by believers who seek to do the will of God in this present godless age.

References to creation outside Genesis (62 in all): Exodus 20:11; Nehemiah 9:6; Job 10:8,9; 26:7-14; 33:4; 38:4-38; Psalms 8:3-9; 19:1-6; 24:1,2; 33:6-9; 74:16,17; 89:11,12; 90:2; 95:5; 100:3; 102:25; 104:5-27; 115:15; 119:73; 121:2; 124:8; 134:3; 136:5-9; 146:6; 148:4,5; Proverbs 8:22-31; 16:4; 17:5; Ecclesiastes 3:11; 7:29; 11:5; Isaiah 40:12,22,28; 42:5; 44:24; 45:7-9; 64:8; Jeremiah 5:22; 10:12; 31:35; 51:15,16; Zechariah 12:1; Matthew 19:4. Mark 10:6. John 1:1-4,10; Acts 4:24; 7:49,50; 14:15; 17:24-28; Romans 1:20; 1 Corinthians 8:6; Ephesians 3:9; Colossians 1:16,17; 3:10; 1 Timothy 4:3,4; Hebrews 1:10; 2:10; James 3:9; 2 Peter 3:5; Revelation 3:14; 4:11; 10:6; 14:7.

"It is written"

"The attitude towards Holy Scripture of a vast deal of cultured thought and responsible teaching at present offers assuredly a problem which it is idle to dismiss as of it were not portentous. By whatsoever process it has come to be, teachers far and wide now regard the Old Testament from an angle totally different from that taken by our Lord Jesus Christ, alike before and after His resurrection from the dead. To Him, tempted, teaching, suffering, dying, risen, 'it is written' was a formula of infinite import. The principle this expressed lay at the heart of His teaching. It is not too much to say that it belonged to the pulse, the vital breath, of His message to others and to His certainty about Himself. But it is now openly or tacitly taken to be out of date, to be narrow, to be uncultured, to make much of 'it is written'; as if it were a thing discredited and to be given up."

These words of Dr Handley Moule, written over 100 years ago, measure the challenge of those who discredit the authority of the Old Testament writings. And he goes on to expose the crucial issue of the controversy in these words: "The conclusion, if true, is a confession that on a matter central in His message our Master was much mistaken, ...with that sort of ignorance which profoundly impairs His whole value as a teacher. Such a fallible Christ lies open to the suspicion of fallibility on other matters than the nature and integrity of the Old Testament". The decisive question in this controversy is, Christ or modern criticism?

2

CHAPTER TWO: THE CREATION OF MAN (JOHN TERRELL)

Creation is the opening word of God's self-revelation to man. Whether we think of the knowledge of God imparted in created things (Romans 1:20) or of the unfolding of Himself in Holy Scripture, the divine initiative in calling the universe into being is paramount. The indictment "that, knowing God, they glorified Him not as God" (Romans 1:21), leaves no doubt concerning human responsibility in regard to the whole of creation; a creation, the plan and execution of which are displayed in the Scriptures in the measure and form determined by God's own wisdom. One obvious element in the plan of creation as recorded in Genesis 1 and 2, is that of movement towards a crowning event - the creation of man.

It is not the purpose of this chapter to explore the field of controversy arising from evolutionary theories. In so far as these are propounded in frank opposition to the concept of a divine creative activity, they present no problem to the Bible-believing Christian. God has spoken in inspired Scripture and declared that, "in the beginning God created ...". There the essential issue rests (John 17:17; Hebrews 11:3). The present purpose is to trace the marvellous act of God in the creation of man in terms of His own purpose of grace, and of the spiritual significance of this divine act. In order to do this, we shall look at the subject under four headings.

The Divine Agent

It is appropriate that we should first focus upon the central place given to the Son. The Scriptures make it clear that, within the work of the Godhead in creation, a unique place is accorded to the Son of God. He is the Creative Word in the prologue of John's Gospel; the Mediator of creative omnipotence in Hebrews 1:2; and the Pre-eminent, the Firstborn of all creation in Colossians 1:15-18. The emphasis, however, on the triune participation in creation comes in Genesis 1:26, where the eternal counsels are revealed in the words, "Let us make man in our image".

This announcement enshrined the message of the total involve-ment of the Godhead; the appearance from the hand of Deity of a creature more fair, more perfect and more responsive by far to Himself than any of the living wanders hitherto produced. In Proverbs 8 the San of Gad is revealed in inspired poetry as the personification of wisdom. As such He is presented in the practical role of "master workman" (vv. 30, 31).

A high note of joy is struck here, "rejoicing always before Him; rejoicing in His habitable earth". This was the day when "the morning stars sang together, and all the sons of God shouted for joy" (Job 38:7). The words which immediately fallow in Proverbs

8:31 have, however, a very special and precious significance for us: "And My delight was with the sons of men". The chosen object of the favour and delight of God the Son was this race of men whose very constitution in the divine "image" promised so much of intelligent communion; such was the outreach of heaven's authority, wisdom and love into this tiny selected planet in the vastness of the universe. Thus, while God in creation, "saw that it was very good", the Master Workman of the Trinity chooses in the subsequent revelation of Scripture to disclose His particular delight in the "sons of men". Although our limited, minds cannot encompass the counsels of Deity from eternity to eternity, yet it is impossible to dissociate the Son's delight from the coming supreme honour which humanity was yet to know when, "she wrapped Him in swaddling clothes, and laid Him in a manger" (Luke 2:7).

The Creative Act

The controversy to which some have been excited by the dual account in Genesis 1 and 2 of the creation of man, is not our concern here. There should be little difficulty in anyone's mind about the complementary character of the two accounts of man's emergence from the hand of God. Of undoubted significance and interest also is the large proportion of the Genesis story of Creation devoted to the making of man. The statement in chapter 1, "and God created man in His own image, in the image of God created He him", seals the truth of man's unique spiritual constitution; of his very special capacity to relate to His Creator. It is associated with God's expressed ambition for man's exercise of delegated authority in this world. This truth is further expounded in the subsequent revelation of

Scripture, which demonstrates more fully the sweet communion which God looked for in man (Genesis 3:8).

We shall return to the matter of man in God's image. What then of Genesis 2:7 - "And the LORD God formed man of the dust of the ground, and breathed into his nostrils the breath of life; and man became a living soul"? This is essentially a biological statement. The man whose body God had formed out of the materials of earth, became "alive".

Yet this does not, surely, exhaust the significance of the passage. No such statement is in fact made about any other living creature which God made. Only on man was the gift of life conferred, we conclude, by such a specific, personally identifying act as "breathed into his nostrils". The uniqueness of this culminating work of creation is underlined for us by the Lord the Spirit. Moreover, the divine record proceeds in some detail to the further activity of the making of a woman from man. Only in the case of man, among living creatures, do we read, "male and female created He them" (1:27). Both sexes were produced, of course, in the animal creation, but it was from man and his new companion that God purposed to illumine the eternal "mystery" of Christ and the Church (Genesis 2:23,24; Ephesians 5:31;32). Thus we can readily appreciate that without man as the apex of the Creator's plan, all else would have been at the best incomplete, and at the worst without point. However, with our God, "His work is perfect" (Deuteronomy 32:4), and the total result of His seven days' work was "very good" (Genesis 1:31).

The Eternal Purpose

Following a little further the matter of the divine purpose in man, touched upon above, we note Paul's declaration to unbelieving men at Athens in Acts 17:28,29. Here, speaking of men as the "offspring of God", he casts their mind back to their divine origin and special relationship to the Creator. Sin and the Fall had intervened, but could never erase the eternal desire of God for fellowship with His creature. The Athenians must raise their eyes above the degrading idolatry into which Satan had deluded them. Not only, however, had the Fall intervened when Paul spoke, but the events of Bethlehem, Calvary and Joseph's garden-tomb had passed into the unfolding history of God's purpose in Man. The incredible had happened; the Creative Word had Himself became flesh (John 1:14). The human spirit is compelled to worship in the face of such a divine intervention. The sheer magnitude of the glory of the Incarnation of God the Son, is overwhelming:

> Woman's Seed in Eden promised,
> God incarnate, virgin-born;
> Morning Star by men unnoticed,
> Herald of a glorious dawn.

It is futile to speculate about this event in relation to God's apparent original purpose for a sinless race on this earth. He who dwells in eternity, who knows the end from the beginning, plans and acts in dimensions of knowledge and purpose not built into the human mind.

Psalm 8 with its central question, "What is man?" (Psalm

8:3,4), intermingles in poetic mystery the divine ambition for man at the first, and the fuller glory of the San of Man in His redemptive suffering and His resurrection supremacy (Hebrews 2:9). Without question, man on earth was central in the eternal plan for representative care and dominion in the chosen planet: "Thou madest him to have dominion over the works of Thy hands". As Erich Sauer has expressed it, "The creation has as its purpose the revelation of the divine glory in the entire life-process of the universe ... On earth this must be achieved in man, God's image, God's representative, and the God-appointed ruler of His creation". Yet in the aftermath of the Fall, an even more glorious purpose comes to light in the taking of "the form of a servant" by Him "who, being in the form of God", was "found in fashion as a Man". And such eternally will God the Son remain the Man in the glory. Which brings us to...

The Final Consummation

The day of the ultimate execution of the righteous sentence upon Adam must have cast deep gloom over the universe, as his aged, worn, and possibly diseased body rested back in death in mother earth. But Paul's very soul must have thrilled in response to the guiding Spirit as he wrote to the Philippians, of Christ, "Who shall fashion anew the body of our humiliation, that it may be conformed to the body of His glory". As we think of God becoming Man our spirits rise yet again to glory in the sorrow and in the triumph of Calvary.

> O sacred Head, what glory,
> What bliss till now was Thine
> Yet, though despised and gory,

> I joy to call Thee mine.
> Thy grief and Thy compassion
> Were all for sinners' gain;
> Mine, mine was the transgression,
> But Thine the deadly pain.

Yes, omniscient Deity had seen the moment of redemption, and the elevation of ruined mankind to eternal glory in Christ. Created in the "image of God" at the first as to his spiritual constitution, an eternity of still fuller dignity, awaits a cleansed and restored race of men.

The Christian has "put on the new man, which is being renewed unto knowledge after the image of Him that created him" (Colossians 3:10). As Paul instructed the Corinthians, "The first man Adam became a living soul. The last Adam became a life-giving Spirit" and, moreover, "as we have borne the image of the earthy, we shall also bear the image of the heavenly" (1 Corinthians 15:45,49). How majestically is the consummation of the counsels of God's grace summed up in Romans 8:29: "For whom He foreknew, He also foreordained to be conformed to the image of His Son, that He might be the Firstborn among many brethren". The Son of God, pre-eminent in creative power and glory, shared with none the pre-eminence "in bringing many sons unto glory" (Hebrews 2:10). "Let us make man" came the voice of the Creator at the first. "What is man?" came the question of the Psalmist before long. "Handle Me and see" said the living Christ in resurrection glory. David must have glimpsed it all, if darkly, to break forth, "O LORD, our Lord, how excellent is Thy name in all the earth!" (Psalm 8:1,9).

3

CHAPTER THREE: THE FALL (GEORGE PRASHER JNR.)

Why the mysterious paradox in human experience? Why in the same generation the noble idealism of a Schweitzer and the depraved philosophy of a Hitler? How could the author of the 23rd Psalm be the murderer of Uriah the Hittite? The problem runs through all human history. The question clamours for an answer. Why the paradox? Human reasoning has offered various explanations - speculative, theoretical, unsatisfactory. The first three chapters of Genesis reveal the cause of the problem - authoritative, in harmony with the facts of known experience.

For Genesis 1:27 summarizes man's unique creation: "God created man in His own image, in the image of God created He him; male and female created He them". As to their wonderful endowments of spirit and intellect, emotion and will, there was reflected in Adam and Eve the image of their Creator. From that noble origin derives all that is admirable in human experience. The inspired narrative of Genesis 3 then discloses the tragedy of

Adam's disobedience, as a result of which all his descendants have been born with a sinful nature (Job 14:1-4; Psalm 51:5; Romans 5:12; John 3:6). So every individual, however noble his ideals or brilliant his achievements, is subject to the mysterious and evil compulsion of "the law of sin" in his members (Romans 7:23). God's answer to the paradox is that He created man perfect in the beginning, but that perfection was marred through rebellion against the divine will. Man therefore "fell" from his original glory and dignity, from the enjoyment of perfect harmony with his Creator.

It was the Son of God Himself who confirmed the truth of Adam and Eve's original creation by directly quoting from Genesis 1:27 - see Mark 10:6 - and also His general confirmation of the truth of Moses' writings (e.g. Luke 24:27,44; John 5:44-47). Apostolic teaching also referred to the first three chapters of Genesis as factual narrative (see Romans 5:12; 1 Corinthians 15:22; 2 Corinthians 11:3; 1 Timothy 2:13-14). Indeed the whole structure of God's redemptive purpose in Christ is built upon the premise that through Adam's disobedience the entire human family became involved in sin and subject to condemnation.

Human history is in itself further confirmation of man's fall. As presented in Scripture, each fresh epoch of God's dealings with men has led only to a climax of increased sinfulness and the need for divine intervention in judgement. The "age of conscience" ended with the Flood; the period after Noah with the judgement of Babel; the dispensation of the law with the scattering of Israel. Following the age of grace will be the high watermark of human iniquity in the person of Antichrist. Even the glory of the millennial age will close in rebellion and summary divine judgement. God puts man to the test under a variety of circumstances, but inevitably the inherent sinfulness of the human heart has resulted in ruinous failure.

Details given by the Holy Spirit in Genesis 3 are replete with truths which run on throughout all Scripture. The sinister personality of Satan, using the serpent through which to communicate with Eve, is seen in his character as a liar and the father of lies (John 8:44). We are left in no doubt about this, for the "old serpent" is identified in Revelation 20:2 with "the Devil and Satan". So the fearful impact of evil on the Adamic race resulted from Satanic initiative in drawing away Adam and Eve from their allegiance to the Creator. Impenetrable mystery enshrouds the earlier origin of sin, although Ezekiel 28 and Isaiah 14 give some indication of Satan's self-exaltation and consequent judgement. But this we see as in a glass darkly. God has not chosen to reveal more fully the origins of evil. His divine wisdom commends to faith's acceptance the plain declaration that "through one man sin entered into the world, and death through sin; and so death passed unto all men, far that all sinned" (Romans 5:12). In each fleeting generation the realities of sin and death confirm the truth of the Fall and explain the dilemma of the human race. Man's deep need is met by God's far-reaching development of His great salvation plan, while from Genesis to Revelation "the god of this world", Satan, is seen to pursue relentlessly his opposing policies.

The adversary's methods in Eden were characteristic. The serpent was more subtle than any beast of the field, so was accordingly chosen as the instrument of deception. The woman was "the weaker vessel" so the approach was made to her. Bible-wide, Satan's ways are stamped with subtlety. "I fear, lest by any means, as the serpent beguiled Eve in his craftiness, your minds should be corrupted from the simplicity and the purity that is toward Christ" (2 Corinthians 11:3). Essentially evil, he nevertheless fashions Himself into an angel of light (2 Corinthians 11:14). At the time of the end the coming of his false Christ will be with "lying wanders, and with all deceit of unrighteousness" (2 Thessalonians 2:9,10). His last mention in Scripture describes his as "the devil that deceived them" (Revelation 20:10).

Typical of his methods also was Satan's successful undermining of Eve's faithfulness to the word of God. It has always been God's way to commit His truth to men to believe and keep, even though they may not fully understand the reason why. The command about the forbidden fruit was definite. It should have been respected. It was a focal point of spiritual proving. Satan effectively lured Eve from her only safe position - to stand in absolute faith in God's statements and obedience to His commands. There would seem to be an element of carelessness in her treatment of God's word if we compare verses 16,17 of chapter 2 with 2,3 of chapter 3. Her quotation in reply to Satan's enquiry added to and altered and took from what God had actually said. There followed Satan's denial of the truth of God's statement: "Thou shalt not surely die". Then came the suggestion that a higher knowledge was being deliberately withheld by God through forbidding them to eat of the fruit. The wide range of philosophy which sets aside Scripture as something less than the inspired ward of God is in essence merely a development of the method used by Satan in Eden.

Eve's decision was partly influenced by the appeal of the fruit to her natural senses - "good for food and ... a delight to the eyes". But there was also an appeal to her mind, far the fruit was to be desired to make one wise. How clearly we can recognize the skill of our adversary in assailing the citadel of the human will! By appeal to bodily appetite, to aesthetic taste and to intellectual attainment he engineered the yielding of Eve's will to his deceitful suggestions. Throughout succeeding centuries he has used a similar pattern of appeal, with the result that for most of mankind life has been "according to the prince of the power of the air", "doing the desires of the flesh and of the mind" (Ephesians 2:3).

There was, of course, same truth in the Devil's statement that Adam and Eve would be as God, knowing good and evil; but it was not wholly truth. They would know good and evil indeed, but not as God knew it. "Instead of perceiving the evil from the free height of the good, he perceived the good from the deep abyss of the evil". We can trace a similar pattern of truth misapplied when Satan tempted the Lord in the wilderness. In that arena of acute spiritual conflict, the last Adam foiled Satan's guile by the power of the written word. In modern spiritual controversy we find this method of Satanic deception widely illustrated. The man of God furnished completely through Spirit-taught understanding of the inspired Scriptures will discern the error despite its wily presentation.

Immediate results of Adam and Eve's disobedience were a consciousness of their need of clothing, and a sense of guilt towards God. They sewed fig leaves together for a covering and hid from the Lord's presence when they heard His voice in the garden. Confronted by God, the guilty pair heard spelt out the solemn consequences of their sin. Yet two rays of hope shone through the gloom of their condemnation. First was the promise that the seed of the woman would bruise the serpent's head. However faintly Adam and Eve may have understood the outworking of this promise, it nevertheless gave them assurance of God's ultimate intervention to retrieve the disaster of the Fall. Secondly we note the clothing of skins provided by God in replacement of the inadequate fig leaves. Enshrined in this act lay the truth that human guilt would be dealt with by the shedding of blood, pointing on to Calvary and the One who would there make propitiation for the sins of the whole world (1 John 2:2).

However, many centuries must pass before the promised Seed would be born in Bethlehem or deal the blow to the serpent's head at Calvary. The history of those centuries ran true to the pattern of judgement pronounced on Adam and Eve. Far the woman there was multiplication of sorrow and conception, sorrow in bringing forth children. The man toiled laboriously because of the cursed ground, until ultimately he returned to the ground; "for dust thou art, and unto dust shalt thou return".

Scripture reveals that the creation over which Adam had been placed was sadly affected by his transgression. His own physical being was itself affected by his spiritual rebellion against God. In a spiritual sense he died when he transgressed; his spiritual communion with God was immediately broken. This was followed in due course by physical death; spiritual death had its physical counterpart. The creation had been placed under his authority (Genesis 1.28). His renunciation of the Creator's authority led to serious consequences throughout the creation of which he was head. As it is put in Romans 8: "The creation was subjected to vanity, not of its own will, but by reason of Him who subjected it, in hope that the creation itself also shall be delivered from the bondage of corruption ... for we know that the whole creation groaneth and travaileth in pain together until now" (vv. 20-22).

As for fallen man, let us face and accept the Bible truth that sin has invaded and spoiled every part of his being, spirit, soul and body. It is a false concept that in every man there is a "spark of the divine", an element of absolute good which may be nurtured for the individual's acceptance by God apart from the redeeming work of Christ. God's word analyses accurately our deep human need as a result of the Fall. As to our body, it is the "body of our humiliation" (Philippians 3:21), subject to the "law of sin" which is in our members (Romans 7:23). As to our thoughts, "the mind of the flesh is death", "the mind of the flesh is enmity against God" (Romans 8:6,7). As to our spiritual capacity, "the natural man receiveth not the things of the Spirit of God: far they are foolishness unto him; and he cannot know them, because they are spiritually judged" (1 Corinthians 2:14). Indeed, all are under sin, as it is written, "There is none righteous, no, not one ... there is none that doeth good, no, not so much as one" (Romans 3:9-12). In such uncompromising terms God describes our state before Him as a result of the Fall and apart from the reclaiming power of His salvation in Christ.

Yet through faith in His Son and by the quickening of the Holy Spirit the regenerate man may dedicate his body as a living sacrifice, holy, acceptable to God (Romans 12.1). He may be spiritually transformed from glory to glory into the image of Christ (2 Corinthians 3:18). He has in prospect the glorious assurance of being conformed to the body of His glory (Philippians 3:21). How wonderfully our all-sufficient Saviour has restored that which He took not away!

4

CHAPTER FOUR: THE FLOOD (LINDSAY PRASHER)

The Holy Spirit's New Testament witness to the Genesis 6 Flood is through three persons:

(1) The Lord Jesus Christ (Matthew 24:38-39; Luke 17:27).

(2) The apostle Peter (1 Peter 3:20; 2 Peter 2:5; 3:5).

(3) The writer of Hebrews (Hebrews 11:7).

Two general principles run through these passages - principles which are important to underline in our own times:

(i) the faith of the righteous is rewarded by God,

(ii) the lack of faith of the unrighteous leads to punishment by God.

Commencing with the Hebrews reference: the faith of Noah is set in striking contrast against the dark background of the faithless degeneration of the rest of the ancient world. His faith was daunted neither by the extent of the impending judgement of God on the unrighteous nor by the size of the task allotted to him, to save alive in one boat the only breathing creatures that would be left in the earth; in this respect the importance of Genesis 6:17 and 7:22 cannot be over-emphasized.

Lesser mortals would have staggered at the construction of a ship the size of QE2, to be stocked with food for a whole year, with the prospect of weathering a flood of the size that God revealed in advance. It is this kind of faith which God rewards equally in today as in B.C. 2418/17, the Bible date of the Flood.

Looking next at Peter's first letter: the Flood is illustrative of the longsuffering of God, giving men every chance before He brought down His judgement. He waited while Noah constructed his huge craft, far greater than anything that had been conceived in his day; waited so that Methuselah ("when he is dead it shall be sent") became the oldest man on record. Side by side with this illustration in the same verse is a very different one: that the Flood is a type of baptism. Just as the earth was completely enveloped in water, so today the Christian who seeks to carry out God's will must comply with the command to be baptized in water.

The second chapter of Peter's second letter throws fresh light on God's waiting: in that period he used Noah as a preacher of righteousness so that his unrighteous contemporaries could have no excuse when God's judgement fell. However, the main issue in the passage is that God brings His faithful ones safely through the punishment reserved for the unbelieving. Like Noah and his family, Christians today rest assuredly on God's ability to do this.

The third chapter of Peter's second letter warns sceptics and scoffers that the uniformity which they think they detect in past history is no security against the reality of God's sudden judgement. This little understood passage needs careful analysis, but one thing is quite evident: the pre-Flood heavens are distinguished from the present heavens, the pre-Flood earth from the present earth, just as much as the pre-Flood world of people from its present inhabitants. The less evident revelation is that it was the pre-Flood heavens and earth which were the cause of the rise in the level of the waters which drowned the ancient inhabitants. Weymouth's translation makes this plain:

"For they are wilfully blind to the fact that there were heavens which existed of old and an earth, the latter arising out of water and extending continuously through water, by the command of God, and that by means of these (margin: i.e. the heavens and earth) the then existing race of men was overwhelmed with water and perished. But the present heavens and the present earth are, by the command of the same God, kept stored up, reserved for fire in preparation for a day of judgement and of destruction for the ungodly".

Though the climate of current scientific opinion favours only local Mesopotamian flooding in association with the considerable layers of water-laid clay at such excavations as Ur, Kish and Shuruppak (Fara), there are acknowledged facts which are irreconcilable with such a limited view. Some of these facts have come into prominence with the change that has occurred since Woolley's time (1929) in the date assigned to the layers and their immediately adjacent strata. Mallowan looks to Early Dynastic II as the period of the Genesis 6 Flood, based chiefly on the Gilgamesh epic and the Sumerian King list. Mallowan's tentative date for Early Dynastic II is B.C. 2700. Radiocarbon dating far the same period is B.C. 2184 but this is known to be too near an assignment, as indicated below. Note that the Bible date falls between these two.

H. W. Catley's report is significant: "We have to infer a serious calamity in Cyprus in the middle of the third millennium B.C. ... it was accompanied by the wholesale desertion of settlements throughout the island: the almost total disappearance of the distinctive features of the Chalcolithic I material culture from the centuries that followed". Moving to higher ground in Israel, the excavations of caves in Mount Carmel by the British School of Archaeology in Jerusalem and the American School of Prehistoric Research have revealed successive layers of deposits, now quite well known. Level B at El Tabun, below the Bronze Age level, was distinguished from all lower layers by the following features:

1. it consisted of red, alluvial, lime-free earth, which it was agreed, could only have been washed in from above, whereas lower layers consisted of brown loam containing lime and conformable with the natural rock of the area.
2. the deposit contained a mixture of animal and human bones and weapons which were distributed "with an un-usual regularity throughout the layer", whereas lower layers contained deliberately buried skeletons.
3. no traces of hearths were visible or other signs of human occupation, which were features of lower layers.
4. the weapons showed no change in human industries asso-ciated with the immediately lower or higher strata.

5. there was clear evidence of an abrupt faunal change to the modern type, whereas lower layers had shown a wider variety of species.

In respect of the last feature, the report states that the abrupt faunal break to present-day species has been recognized in many deposits in Europe, North Africa and East Africa. "This seems to suggest it may have been contemporary over a very wide area". Hopwaad has confirmed this in Africa and also India and states "that some major geological event must have so affected the general conditions over a far wider area than Europe, that the greater part of the faunas became extinct, leaving an impoverished remnant behind". He shows that these extinctions were accompanied by widespread earth movements, including mountain formation "very late in the Pleistocene period". By inference Bate associates this period with level B at El Tabun.

A study has been made of bone and alluvial deposits in caves and fissures in many parts of the world at the same geological horizon, and the evidence is overwhelmingly great that they represent the remains of animals - and humans - drowned in a flood of vast dimensions. Bones are not eroded; they are well-preserved, whereas those of many diverse species, predatory and otherwise, are all mixed together.

So much for earth movements and their consequences; but what of movements in the heavens, of which Peter spoke? The anomalous radiocarbon dating in the middle of the third millennium B.C., noted above in relation to the second early Dynastic period, has been attributed by Mallowan to "a major disturbance, which changed the balance of C14 in the atmosphere". An attractive mechanism, that of the loss of a vapour canopy, has been suggested by several to account for the change, because this would cause a sudden influx of cosmic rays from space and have the effect noted above by an "overshoot" mechanism. Dates nearer to the present than the major disturbance would appear to be falsely nearer still, and dates farther from the present than the disturbance would appear falsely more distant, and this is exactly the problem which archaeologists are faced with.

Clearly no one of the above pieces of evidence alone would carry convincing weight, but the patient seeker after truth finds them in agreement with the evidence relative to tree ring dating, population statistics, frozen mammoth deposits in Siberia and Alaska and other equally diverse fields of investigation. However, the words of the Lord Jesus form a fitting conclusion to this brief survey of New Testament references to the Genesis 6 Flood. He used the deluge as a type of His judgement of the world at His coming as Son of Man. He said that Flood "took them all away" (Matthew 24:39), "destroyed them all" (Luke 17:27). Such all-embracing statements, completely in accord with the Old Testament record, cannot lightly be set aside or ignored.

5

CHAPTER FIVE: THE SCATTERING AT BABEL (TOM HYLAND)

In previous chapters, we have traced the early history of man from his creation and fall to the Flood. It is a sad and shameful story. So rapidly and completely did the human family become corrupted by sin that there was no alternative but devastating judgement. Thus ended the first great epoch in human history: "God ... spared not the ancient world, but ... brought a flood upon the world of the ungodly" (2 Peter 2:4,5).

But God was bound by promise to send a Deliverer who would crush Adam's conqueror (Genesis 3:15), so He "preserved Noah with seven others" and moved forward to the next stage in His great plan of redemption. Each stage of that plan was a divine initiative and was fiercely contested by His great adversary, Satan. God, however, was always a move ahead. The Eden promise was the pledge of the triune Jehovah, resting for its execution in His unerring wisdom, power and love. The details of the plan would unfold gradually through the millenniums of human history.

After the waters of the Flood had subsided, God made a covenant with Noah and his sons. A new age had begun. The special features of the Noachian covenant were:

1. An assurance that the present earth would be preserved for the fulfilment of God's saving purpose: "While the earth remaineth, seedtime and harvest, and cold and heat, and summer and winter, and day and night shall not cease" (Genesis 8:22).
2. Man's authority over nature was re-affirmed but not in its original majesty as enjoyed by Adam in his unfallen state. Fear, not deference, would be the basis of man's lordship aver the animal world.
3. Governmental powers for mankind were authorized. Violence was to be restrained by the introduction of capital punishment for the murderer.
4. The rainbow was set in the clouds as the sign of divine faithfulness.

It was clearly the divine intention that as mankind multiplied after the Flood they should disperse and occupy various territories in the earth according to their ethnic affinities. There were to be three main divisions of the human family, descending from each of the sons of Noah: Shem, Ham and Japheth. The plan for this dispersal is laid down in Genesis chapter 10. Students of ancient history have given close study to this remarkable chapter which, according to Canon G. Rawlinson, M.A., is "the earliest ethnographical essay" extant. We do not attempt to examine in detail the divine plan for the dispersal of mankind. Our principal concern in this chapter is to view the scattering at Babel in the wider concept of God's dealings with men.

The attempt by mankind to frustrate God's plan that they should spread abroad in the earth (Genesis 11:1-9) is the outstanding event in this period of man's history. It reveals that when entrusted with governmental authority men proceeded to unite in rebellion against their Creator. The plain in the land of Shinar was the site of this daring act of defiance. There the first post-deluvian city was founded and the great tower, the symbol of mankind's political aspirations, was devised. The intention is clearly indicated: "And they said, Go to, let us build us a city, and a tower, whose top may reach unto heaven, and let us make us a name; lest we be scattered abroad upon the face of the whole earth" (Genesis 11:4).

Sad indeed! The corruption of man's nature through sin, demonstrated in the moral collapse which incurred the judgement of the Flood, now manifested itself in organized rebellion against God. Man aspired to develop a society of his own devising, with God outside. What madness! Yet the delusion of which Babel was the germ has been fostered throughout the ages of human history. It has brought great civilizations to ruin; it is one of the most convincing external proofs of the exceeding sinfulness of sin.

But in spite of man's affront, God was still at work for his eventual blessing. He had already chosen the location where He would work out His redeeming purpose - a coastal strip of land at the eastern end of the Mediterranean Sea. God's plan for the post-deluvian epoch was to divide mankind into nations and spread them out around this centre. The significance of this divine preparatory operation is expressed by Moses in his inspired song:

"When the Most High gave to the nations their inheritance,
    When He separated the children of men,
    He set the bounds of the peoples
    According to the number of the children of Israel"
    (Deuteronomy 32:8).

This divine commentary on the events recorded in Genesis 10 and 11 reveals, (1) that the land allocated to each of the nations was an inheritance from the Most High, and (2) that there was divine control; the bounds of the peoples being set in relation to the number of the children of Israel - a nation as yet unborn. God's chosen people would eventually occupy a land which, geographically and politically, would be the hub of His purposes for this earth. (Note Ezekiel 38:12, where the land of Israel is described as "the middle of the earth".) To that land and from that people, in the fulness of time, the Redeemer would come to fulfil the Eden promise.

The attempt to frustrate God's plan for the dispersal of mankind in the earth was Satan-inspired; an early counter-move by His adversary. It was futile. God thwarted it, not by an overt act of judgement but by the simple means of the confusion of tongues. This proved a most effective method of bringing their project to an ignoble end: "So the LORD scattered them abroad from thence upon the face of all the earth: and they left off to build the city. Therefore was the name of it called Babel; because the LORD did there confound the language of all the earth" (Genesis 11:8,9).

From a cursory reading of Genesis chapter 11 it might be con-strued that the scattering at Babel was indiscriminate and that mankind drifted wherever they would. This is clearly not the case. There was divine overruling. The movement of mankind followed the plan laid down by God in Genesis chapter 10.

As we have already observed, the 'Babel' idea has persisted throughout human history, and ungodly men down the ages have been enamoured with it. The Hebrew word for 'Babel' (elsewhere translated, Babylon) stands in Scripture as the symbol of human federation in opposition to God. The first great ungodly leader to found a kingdom by conquest with this in view was Nimrod: "Nimrod ... began to be a mighty one in the earth. He was a mighty hunter before the LORD ... And the beginning of his kingdom was Babel" (Genesis 10:8-10).

This, of course, was not the unfinished city of Genesis 11: "As the Babel builders, when their speech was confounded, were scattered abroad, and therefore deserted both the city and the tower which they commenced to build, Babylon as a city could not properly be said to exist till Nimrod, by establishing his power there, made it the foundation and the starting point of his greatness" (Hislop). The last great rebellion against God and His Christ will take place in the same area (Revelation 16:12-21). The movement which began so long ago in the plain of Shinar will reach its zenith in the great political-commercial-religious combine at the end-time. The apostle John saw its final destruction in vision: "Babylon the great was remembered in the sight of God, to give unto her the cup of the wine of the fierceness of His wrath" (Revelation 16:19).

We have now covered the first eleven chapters of Genesis. In this small space we are given a condensed record of man's early history, and the first steps God took to retrieve the tragedy of the Fall. The record is unmistakably endorsed by the testimony of our Lord in the days of His flesh. The divine purpose in giving us this history at the beginning of His word is clear. He has been at work for man's redemption ever since "the reign of sin began". Nothing will deflect Him from it. Man is in bondage to sin. He is not only incapable of self-redemption but has no desire to be freed from his bondage. Further, as this early record shows, he has allowed himself to be led by Satan to oppose God's saving purpose. All this exposes the fearfulness of his fall, and shows that he can only be saved from its consequences by divine grace.

As we view the history of salvation from its early beginnings to its glorious consummation we can but reiterate Paul's fervent doxology: "O the depth of the riches both of the wisdom and the knowledge of God! How unsearchable are His judgements, and His ways past tracing out ... For of Him, and through Him, and unto Him, are all things. To Him be the glory for ever. Amen" (Romans 11:33,36).

6

CHAPTER SIX: THE CALL OF ABRAM (J.A. LENNOX BROWN)

Why did God call Abram? Was there an intrinsic something in the man which attracted the Lord's attention? It is evident from the Scriptures that God does not act on whims but is governed by principles. It is also clear that because of this the Lord is no respecter of persons. Some men have attained a marvellously close rapport with God. But in every case it was the result of that person's heart response to the voice of God to him.

All we know of Abram before the Call, is his family tree. But we can assume that during his life he had rejected Chaldean religious philosophy, had acknowledged the Lord as the one true God, and had established a one-to-one relationship with God. It is inconceivable that the Call came to a wealthy, idol worshipping heathen, out of a clear blue sky.

Before we examine the "why" of the Call; it is utterly thrilling to observe its effects. The Lord said "Get thee out ..." (Genesis 12:1). "So Abram went, as the LORD had spoken unto him" (v.4). This is one of the great examples of instant obedience. No arguments, no excuses, no pleas for time, no reservations just "Abram went". The standards of our time and society allow us to rationalize almost any position we care to take. And invariably it is easy to give cogent reasons for not fully obeying the word of the Lord to me right now. Abram did not rationalize.

So why did God call Abram? From Genesis 12:2,3, we see seven direct consequences which God stated would flow out of Abram's obedience to the Call:

(1) "I will make of thee a great nation, and
(2) I will bless thee,
(3) and make thy name great;
(4) and be thou a blessing:
(5) and I will bless them that bless thee,
(6) and him that curseth thee will I curse:
(7) and in thee shall all the families of the earth be blessed".

It is blessing all the way: and blessing in an ever-widening circle, like a stone thrown into the water. The ripples move outwards to the farthest bank. God called Abram to bless the world. Yes, that is the crux of it. "All the families of the earth" - is total coverage both in time and in geography. When God laid hold of Abram on that ancient day in the city of Ur, He was loving you and me. He was "so loving" the world.

Everything that lies between the call to Abram and the ultimate blessing of all is, in the complete overview of things, only incidental. One must not belittle the significance of the Israel nation and the divine law which was given to that nation. Neither must we discount the importance in God's purposes of great men who milestone the history of Israel; Abram himself under his new name Abraham; Jacob, Moses, Samuel, David and scores of others. But the Israelite nation was not an end in itself. And the great men of the race were not complete in themselves. God blessed the nation, as He had promised, and He blessed the men of the nation. He judged the nations that cursed Israel and blessed them that sided with the Lord's people.

But the great end in view in all this was Christ. Christ, the Seed of Abraham (Galatians 3:16); the One through whom all things would be reconciled to God (Colossians 1.20); who came to take away the sin of the world (John 1:29); the Person in whom all things in the heavens and upon the earth would be summed up (Ephesians 1:10).

Paul argued strongly to the Galatians that they were receiving the "blessing of Abraham in Christ Jesus" but had been bewitched into a denial of the blessing and the glorious liberty it brings in the Spirit. The "blessing of Abraham" means the blessing of God to us all through Abraham and his Seed, which is Christ. The blessing of God has from time to time squeezed through the narrow channel of one man. It was so with Noah and with Abraham. Let us, the many who have the blessing, praise God for the faithful few through whom it passed to reach us in overflowing fulness in the Person of our Saviour Himself.

The call of Abram and the promises contained in it are suggestively illustrative of the call today to believers on the Lord Jesus Christ. It has been said that there is more than one call given by God to men today. It is evident that there are calls within calls. Paul was "called to be an apostle of Jesus Christ" (1

Corinthians 1:1). This was a very special vocation. But there is clearly God's call through the gospel, to which every believer has responded. We are vessels of mercy prepared by God so that He might make known the riches of His glory. So He called us, not from the Jews only, but also from the Gentiles (Romans 9:23,24). Peter reminds us that we were called "out of darkness into His marvellous light" (1 Peter 2:9).

So Abram was called to leave relationships and an environment which represented total spiritual darkness. He was to move into a new land to be clothed with the brightness of divine blessing. This was to be the centre of God's plan for the world. Here would grow a powerful nation, thriving under the blessing of divine rule and, in turn, blessing the nations around. Only continuing obedience to the terms of the call and belief in the promises associated with it were required. We all know the chequered history of God's chosen nation, reaching its zenith during the reign of Solomon and its nadir when the Lord Jesus pronounced desolation on the house. But through all the vagaries of this history the royal line was preserved and in the fulness of time God sent forth His Son born of a woman. And Mary laid her first-born baby in a manger. The Seed of Abraham had come.

The seven promises of God when he called Abram contain an exhortation and a prediction. The exhortation was: "be thou a blessing". The prediction was: "in thee shall all the families of the earth be blessed". The exhortation and the prediction go hand-in-hand for the Lord's people today.

Just as Israel was not an end in itself; neither are we. Paul outlined to Titus the great redemptive purpose of Christ with a view to purifying unto Himself "a people for His own possession, zealous of good works" (Titus 2:14). To the Ephesians he said: "We are His workmanship, created in Christ Jesus for good works, which God afore prepared that we should walk in them" (Ephesians 2:10). Peter corroborates these statements when he expresses the purpose of an elect race, a royal priesthood, a holy nation, a people for God's own possession as being the showing forth of "the excellencies of Him who called you out of darkness into His marvellous light" (1 Peter 2:9). God is the antithesis of selfishness.

His wanting a people for His own possession is not the kind of acquisitive urge which is the hallmark of the materialist. It is a step, a vital step, in His mighty redemptive plan, to reach the world through His people, to show His love and mercy and glory through the redeemed of the Lord. This is the mission of the people of God, and to miss or neglect it is to abort the plan of God for His people. The essence of this message is that worship and witness are indivisible: neglect of one distorts the whole. Ecclesiastical history from Pentecost to date is clear evidence of this.

> "For Abraham who Thee believed,
> And glorious promises received;
> The friend of God; our father he,
> Who follow him in trusting Thee;
> We give Thee thanks."

7

CHAPTER SEVEN: ABRAHAM OFFERS UP ISAAC (GEORGE PRASHER SNR.)

There are two landmarks in this story: the first, Beersheba, where Abraham was dwelling; and the second, Moriah, to which place Abraham was sent. Beersheba means the well of the oath, and Moriah the vision of Jah. The wells in Palestine were mostly springs, and Beersheba takes our thoughts to the past eternity where God's love for man was surging in His bosom.

When Isaiah heard the voice of the LORD saying, "Whom shall I send, and who will go for us?", he replied, "Here am I; send me" (Isaiah 6:8). This, we judge, was a faint re-echo from a remote "Beersheba" when God planned the great work of redemption. Because of the vastness of that work none save One from the Godhead was eligible, since He must meet the claims of divine justice on the one hand, and the need of a ruined race on the other. So we judge we can hear the Son of God saying, "Here am I; send Me". Moriah, the vision of Jah, where Abraham was sent to sacrifice his son, was where God's temple was built in later years with its altar of sacrifice. Outside that city wall at the place called Calvary the Son of God was slain as He bore the penalty of our sin, and made atonement through His blood. This was all foreshadowed in the journey of Abraham and Isaac from Beersheba to Moriah.

God did prove Abraham

God commanded, "Take now thy son, thine only son, whom thou lovest, even Isaac, and get thee into the land of Moriah; and offer him there for a burnt offering upon one of the mountains which I will tell thee of" (Genesis 22:2). These words show how fully God had entered into the trial He was giving Abraham. It has been remarked had God only said, 'Take now thy son', Abraham could have replied, 'But he is my only son'. Had God said, 'Take thine only son', he might have pleaded, 'But I love him'; and had God stopped there Abraham might have continued to plead, 'He is my Isaac, which means laughter, my joy'. But God had considered all this and so framed His command that no way of escape, or room to parry, was left.

Obedience of faith

The Psalmist says, "I made haste, and delayed not, to observe Thy commandments" (Psalm 119:60), and thus it was with Abraham. He "rose early in the morning, and saddled his ass, and took two of his young men with him, and Isaac his son … and rose up, and went unto the place of which God had told him". He might have thought it well to reconsider the matter, but this was not the way with Abraham the friend of God. It was enough that God had spoken. Though the task appointed him pierced his soul, he rose early in the morning, cleaving the wood and preparing for the long journey to Moriah.

The assurance of faith

The third day brought the place of sacrifice within sight, though still afar off. Here the company was divided, the young men and the ass being left behind, while the father and the son went on together. "I and the lad will go yonder", said Abraham, "and we will worship, and come again to you". As the Lord Jesus was nearing the cross He testified, "I am not alone, because the Father is with Me" (John 16:32). And again, "He that sent Me is with Me; He hath not left Me alone" (8:29). Thus the Father and the Son were going on together. Even while being nailed to the cross the Lord Jesus could speak to His Father - and say, "Father, forgive them; for they know not what they do" (Luke 23:34); but darker hours of deeper woe lay ahead, as from the sixth hour "a darkness came over the whole land until the ninth hour", and the Son of God was forsaken by His God, and He cried, "My God, My God, why hast Thou forsaken Me?"

Resemblances and contrasts appear as we proceed with Abraham. The wood for the offering was laid on Isaac, and here we see in shadow our Saviour carrying His cross. But what a contrast! Isaac was fit and fresh and ready for the load he bore; but the prophetic word says of Christ: "The plowers plowed upon My back; they made long their furrows" (Psalm 129:3). The rough heavy cross must have inflicted grievous pain, till at last, we judge, He sank beneath its weight. Abraham carried the fire and the knife - the knife to slay, the fire to consume. In the burnt offering the fire released the sweet savour of the offering.

Where is the lamb?

This question, Where is the lamb? was pressing on Isaac's mind, and it must have rent the heart of Abraham as he gave expression to it. Wisely he replied, "God will provide Himself the lamb for a burnt offering, my son". Arriving at the place which God had told him of, Abraham built the altar, laid the wood in order, and bound Isaac his son. "And Abraham stretched forth his hand, and took the knife to slay his son. And the angel of the LORD called unto him out of heaven, and said ... 'Lay not thine hand upon the lad, neither do thou anything unto him; for now I know that thou fearest God, seeing thou hast not withheld thy son, thine only son, from Me'. And Abraham lifted up his eyes, and looked, and behold, behind him a ram caught in the thicket by his horns: and Abraham went and took the ram, and offered him up for a burnt offering in the stead of his son".

Why was Isaac spared?

An aged friend of mine was seated in a café in his home town at a meal. From a table nearby a Jewish acquaintance called to him, "Mr M., why was Abraham not allowed to sacrifice Isaac?" This was perhaps a rather difficult question, but he replied, "I think it was because Isaac was a sinner, like all other men". This was certainly the correct answer. Each one of us is blighted by sin. Another, a sinless Person, must die for us. This One, the Lord Jesus Christ, "gave Himself a ransom for all; the testimony to be borne in its own times" (1 Timothy 2:5,6). He is typified in the ram that was slain instead of Isaac.

The Lamb of God for sinners died,

A Victim on the tree;
He gave Himself a Sacrifice,
To set the guilty free.
Happy indeed are all who can truly say,
I seek no other argument,
I want no other plea,
It is enough that Jesus died
And rose again for me.

Jehovah-jireh

"And Abraham called the name of that place Jehovah-jireh", which means, 'the LORD will see, or provide'. Yes, though many centuries came and went, the glad morning dawned when a virgin "brought forth her firstborn Son; and she wrapped Him in swaddling clothes, and laid Him in a manger, because there was no room for them in the inn". For 30 years this glorious Person moved in obscurity till the time of His manifestation to Israel. John the Baptist's testimony concerning Him was crystal clear: His own testimony lucid and forceful, yet Jew and Gentile rushed Him to the death of the cross. There the spotless Lamb of God who knew no sin was made sin for us, "that we might become the righteousness of God in Him" (2 Corinthians 5:21). God had seen to this matter, the Lamb had been provided. "All we like sheep have gone astray; we have turned every one to his own way; and the LORD hath laid on Him the iniquity of us all" (Isaiah 53:6).

A Substitute

The cords that had bound Isaac upon the altar were cut, and likely the same knife was used to slay the ram. Isaac would stand beside the altar and witness the ram slain in his stead. So the believer in the Lord Jesus Christ can view by faith the cross of Christ and say with the apostle Paul, "the Son of God, who loved me, and gave Himself up for me" (Galatians 2:20).

Beneath an eastern sky,
Amid a rabble cry,
A Man goes forth to die,
For me.
Thorn-crowned His blessed head,
Blood-stained His every tread,
Crossladen, on He sped,
For me.

Because thou hast obeyed

The obedience of Abraham in this supreme test gave God intense delight. It was proof of his faith that at the command of Jehovah he was ready to slay his son whom he loved so dearly. So God called unto him a second time saying, "Because thou hast done this thing, and hast not withheld thy son, thine only son; that in blessing I will bless thee, and in multiplying I will multiply thy seed as the stars of heaven, and as the sand which is upon the sea shore; and thy seed shall possess the gate of his enemies; and in thy seed shall all the nations of the earth be blessed; because thou hast obeyed My voice". It is significant that God uses both stars and sands to express the countless numbers of

Abraham's offspring. Does the sand upon the sea shore set forth the multitudes of his earthly offspring, and the stars of heaven the myriads reached and blessed through the message of the cross of Christ? So it appears to me.

8

CHAPTER EIGHT: JACOB AND ESAU (ALAN TOMS)

The story of Jacob and Esau commences before their birth, for to their enquiring mother Rebekah who sought from the Lord an explanation for the struggling within her womb, God said,

"Two nations are in thy womb,
  And two peoples shall be separated even from thy bowels:
  And the one people shall be stronger than the other people;
  And the elder shall serve the younger."
(Genesis 25:23)

We are introduced immediately to the profound subject of divine election to which Paul addressed himself in Romans, chapter 9. He carried great sorrow and unceasing pain in his heart on account of his brethren, his kinsmen according to the flesh. Because of their rejection of the Christ they had been set aside "until the fulness of the Gentiles be come in". But in setting them aside God had not broken His word. His promise had not failed. For as Paul pointed out, of Abraham's two sons, it was

Isaac, the son born of promise, who was chosen. "The children of the promise are reckoned for a seed". And if some might have argued that there was good cause for God to choose Isaac because he was the son of Abraham's own wife, whereas Ishmael was the son of the handmaid, Paul hastened to show that of Isaac's two sons, born of the same mother, and indeed of one conception, God made choice of the younger rather than the elder. It is God's prerogative to choose whom He will. He has a purpose in election. Before the boys were born and had therefore an opportunity of doing either good or bad, He declared that the elder would serve the younger.

"Not of works, but of him that calleth"

Isaac, in the weakness of the flesh, and for such a paltry reason as his love for Esau's savoury meat, would have reversed God's order. Rebekah perceiving this, and understanding the purpose of God in regard to her younger son, schemed with Jacob to counter Isaac's move. Doubtless her motive was right, but in her impatience she was interfering where she ought not. God did not require her help in working out his purposes.

Genesis chapter 27 is a sad tale of human failure, impatience and deceit, but over it all we discern the over-ruling hand of God working everything according to His will, for "the purpose of God according to election" must stand. Nothing could alter the divine choice. "I will have mercy on whom I have mercy, and I will have compassion on whom I have compassion" God said to Moses, and that is the "I will" of Deity which no human being can withstand. "So then it is not of him that willeth" strong though Isaac's will was, "nor of him that runneth" fast though

Esau ran, "but of God that hath mercy" (Romans 9:16).

It should be said in passing that although Isaac failed so lamentably in not bowing to the will of God, yet when the deceitfulness was exposed and he realised that God had overruled in causing him to bless his younger son, he refused to go back on the blessing he had pronounced. Trembling exceedingly though he was, he understood that he had spoken oracularly, and in a magnificent burst of faith, to which Hebrews 11:20 doubtless refers, he said, "Yea, and he shall be blessed".

"The elder shall serve the younger"

Therein lies a divine principle, for "that is not first which is spiritual, but that which is natural; then that which is spiritual" (1 Corinthians 15:46). God could as easily have caused Jacob to be born first, but he came forth after his brother that he might be a type of the second Man who is of heaven. And the second Man from heaven came to impart a heavenly nature to those of Adam's sons who would believe on Him, and that new nature in the purposes of God is to have the ascendancy over the old nature. As Paul puts it in describing his own glorious experience, "I have been crucified with Christ; yet I live; and yet no longer I, but Christ liveth in me" (Galatians 2:20).

The character of the two boys was evident from their birth, for Esau "came forth red" or "ruddy", the word coming from the same root as the word "Adam", and he proved to be a man who lived to satisfy the desires of the fallen nature inherited from his first father. Jacob came forth with his hand upon Esau's heel, for which he earned the name supplanter. His supplanting nature drove him at times to acts of cunning and deceitfulness for which he paid dearly in later life. He lived to prove that "whatsoever a man soweth that shall he also reap", for in his manhood he was deceived by his own sons.

"But I loved Jacob" (Malachi 1:2) is the divine decree and deep in the heart of this man whom God loved was a high regard for divine things. He loved what God loved, and with such men and women God is ever prepared to work in His gentleness and patience until He has eradicated the works of the old nature and produced the fruit of the new. After years of deceiving and being deceived, God brought him to Peniel and there, a broken man at last, he emerged a prince with God, as his new name Israel implied. "In his manhood he had power with God" (Hosea 12:3).

"The boys grew"

And as they grew their characters developed along the lines indicated by their early traits. The open life of the field suited the restless nature of Esau which was opposed to all restraint; whereas Jacob with his love for divine things was content to dwell in tents, as were Abraham and Isaac, the heirs with him, or he with them, of the same promise. Yes, Jacob was of the line of faith. He was elected to that, but what he was elected to, he personally grasped by his own faith.

Esau, on the other hand, was a profane man (Hebrews 12:16). He treated sacred things as though they were common. It is not surprising therefore that he so easily parted with his birthright. He sold the spiritual for the material, and as though to stress to human hearts for all time how poor was the bargain, he obtained in exchange a mere mess of pottage. But however much he might have obtained it would have been a bad bargain still, for who can weigh the value of spiritual things against material gain? "The things which are seen are temporal; but the things which are not seen are eternal". Herein the two brothers stand greatly in contrast the one to the other. Esau saw only what was near. The tangible and transient things of time filled his vision, whereas Jacob with the long distance view of faith, saw beyond to the spiritual and eternal. This was the man who obtained the blessing which went with the birthright. Yes, and he was blessed, with the dew of heaven, and the fulness of the earth, and plenty of corn and wine. And as God intends with every blessing which he imparts, it reached out to others, for "blessed be everyone that blesseth thee".

After Jacob fled at the wrath of his brother, over twenty years passed before we read of them together again, and then only for a very short time. Jacob who went out alone returned with two companies, eloquent testimony to the blessing of God upon him. But his strength did not lie in his two companies. That would have been poor defence against Esau with 400 men, and when he heard that his brother was on his way to meet him he was greatly afraid and distressed. But the Lord had foreseen Jacob's distress and at Mahanaim the angels of God met him. He had a glimpse of God's "two hosts or companies", and with that strengthening vision still fresh in his mind he poured out his heart to God in the lovely prayer of Genesis 32: 9-12.

Reverently reminding God of His promises, "I will do thee good ... I will surely do thee good", he pleaded for deliverance from the hand of his brother Esau. And the Lord of the heavenly hosts proved Himself once again to be also the God of a poor, struggling man like Jacob. And do not all who take refuge in the Lord find great comfort in that lovely couplet which came from the pen of the sons of Korah, "The LORD of hosts is with us; The God of Jacob is our refuge" (Psalm 46:7,11)?

"God hath dealt graciously with me"

These two men, whose interests were so different and whose paths lay so far apart, met once again, and to Jacob, who described himself as not worthy of the least of God's mercies, was added yet another mercy, that his brother Esau met him in peace. (Only once more do we read of their paths crossing and that was when family ties brought them together at Isaac's death). It was a momentous meeting, and in the words which they spoke to one another is emphasized once again the unalterable fact that the man who gains most and gains eternally is the man who sets his sights upon God's holy things. As Jacob urged his brother to receive his gift, Esau said, "I have enough; my brother, let that thou hast be thine". But Jacob gave for his reason, as he pressed him again, "because God hath dealt graciously with me, and because I have enough" or "all" as the Hebrew word indicates. Jacob, the man of faith had all. "All things are yours; whether Paul, or Apollos, or Cephas, or the world, or life, or death, or things present, or things to come; all are yours; and ye are Christ's; and Christ is God's" (1 Corinthians 3:21-23).

This lesson cannot be too strongly emphasized, for the spiritual is still being sold for the material, and perhaps never more so than in the days in which we live. Affluence brings an abundance of material things and the great Adversary does not miss his opportunity of trying to turn the disciple's affection from Christ to things. But the timeless words of the Master echo down the centuries of time, warning us that "a man's life consisteth not in the abundance of the things which he possesseth." Riches are deceitful, the Lord Jesus taught. Let us not be deceived by them, or allow them to grip our hearts. Many have reached after earthly gain only to find that they have been led astray from the faith and have pierced themselves through with many sorrows. Esau had his sorrows, and he shed his tears, too - but they came too late. When he afterward desired to inherit the blessing, he was rejected (for he found no place of repentance), though he sought it diligently with tears" (Hebrews 12:17). Let all who value divine things take heed.

9

CHAPTER NINE: JACOB AND THE HOUSE OF GOD (R. LINDSAY)

It must have been with a heavy heart that Jacob left his father's household and began the long journey from Canaan to Paddanaram. The deception practised on Isaac, by which Jacob had supplanted Esau in obtaining the blessing of the firstborn, had aroused his brother's anger, and it was to avoid the consequences of this that Rebekah engineered the departure of her younger son. To the casual eye, the entire episode would suggest nothing more than a chance journey hastily embarked on. But the student of Scripture sees in it the guiding hand of God.

And, when Jacob "lighted upon a certain place" (Genesis 28:11) we can have no doubt that, in His development of the life-pattern of one destined to fill a prime role in the unfolding of His purposes, the LORD brought Jacob to this place. Here awaited an experience which would mark the rest of his life, and here God would for the first time reveal certain fundamental principles in His dealings with men.

That night, Jacob slept beneath the stars, "and he dreamed, and behold a ladder set up on the earth, and the top of it reached to heaven: and behold the angels of God ascending and descending on it. And, behold, the LORD stood above it". What a vision for the lonely traveller! Here was a place in which communion with heaven could be maintained. Most important of all, here was a place in which was the presence of the LORD. "Surely" said Jacob as he awoke, "the LORD is in this place; and I knew it not ... This is none other but the house of God, and this is the gate of heaven". Thus there came to Jacob the first revelation of a truth which looms large in Scripture - that the mighty Creator of all seeks on earth a dwelling place. "And he called the name of that place Bethel: but the name of the city was Luz at the first".

Bethel - house of God among men

This truth is one of the precious threads which run through God's dealings with men in all dispensations. The godly have always marvelled at it. Solomon, in his prayer at the dedication of his temple spoke for all generations, "Will God in very deed dwell on the earth? Behold, heaven and the heaven of heavens cannot contain Thee; how much less this house that I have builded!" (1 Kings 8:27). Yet there can be no doubt that it has always been the desire of God's heart to find a dwelling-place among His people. This was true as He brought Israel out of Egypt. When Moses was called to spend forty days in the mount, he was given, in minute detail, the pattern of the house which Israel must prepare for the LORD. "Let them make Me a sanctuary; that I may dwell among them", said God (Exodus 25:8). And as that erring people journeyed through the desert, the token of His presence among them was ever visible in the pillar which hung over the tabernacle - cloud by day and fire by night.

We have already mentioned that Solomon built for God a house of unparalleled splendour. Likewise, when the remnant of Israel returned from the captivity in Babylon, part of the divine charge to them was, "Go up to the mountain, and bring wood, and build the house; and I will take pleasure in it, and I will be glorified, saith the LORD" (Haggai 1:8). The tent of skins, the splendid building raised by Solomon, and the structure of remnant days all testify that God delighted to dwell among His people.

Today, He still has this desire. Now, "He, being Lord of heaven and earth, dwelleth not in temples made with hands" (Acts 17:24). Churches of God, formed according to the New Testament pattern and built together to form a united testimony, provide God's house on earth today. "Each several building, fitly framed together, groweth into a holy temple in the Lord; in whom ye also are builded together for a habitation of God in the Spirit" (Eph. 2:21,22).

A dreadful place

The realization that, in Bethel, he was in the presence of God filled Jacob with awe. "He was afraid, and said, 'How dreadful is this place!'" Jacob knew the fear of the LORD, and by that fear his conduct in Bethel was thereafter governed. In His later dealings with the nation of Israel, the LORD made clear that the reverence due to His name must be shown also to His house, "Ye shall keep My sabbaths, and reverence My sanctuary: I am the LORD", He said (Leviticus 19:30) and so the godly Israelite approached the house of God in a duly reverent manner. David gave an example of this: "In Thy fear will I worship toward Thy holy temple" (Psalm 5:7) Here surely is a lesson for us. Did not Paul write to Timothy, "That thou mayest know how men ought to behave themselves in the house of God which is the church of the living God"? (1 Timothy 3:15) Our reverence for the name of our God must reflect itself in holy behaviour within His house.

Human instrumentality

It is a key principle in divine revelation that the house of God is built by human instrumentality, and in Jacob's activity in Bethel we see the first expression of this principle. For he "rose up early in the morning and took the stone ... and set it up for a pillar, and poured oil upon the top of it". Later, in the building of the tabernacle, this principle was further developed, as the LORD outlined to Moses the part which would be played by men such as Bezalel, alongside whom worked "every wisehearted man, in whom the LORD hath put wisdom and understanding to know how to work all the work for the service of the sanctuary" (Exodus 36:1).

Centuries after, "Solomon built Him a house" (Acts 7:47). And when, after the captivity in Babylon, a remnant of God's people were once again in the land, "The LORD stirred up the spirit of Zerubbabel ... the spirit of Joshua ..., and the spirit of all the remnant of the people; and they came and did work in the house of the LORD of hosts, their God" (Haggai 1:14). Surely, the teaching is clear. The house of God has always been built and maintained through a God-given exercise of godly men. "Let them make Me a sanctuary that I may dwell among them" still points the way to service which is according to His will.

The stone raised up by Jacob was set up to be a pillar - a place of witness. We are reminded again of Paul's comment to Timothy (1 Timothy 3:15), that the house of God is "pillar and ground of the truth". In the last days, so powerfully described by the apostle in 2 Timothy 3, one of the distinguishing characteristics is the failure of men to come to the knowledge of the truth. They "will not endure sound doctrine". Nevertheless, the witness to the truth of God must be maintained with vigilance. Those in His house must "be instant in season, out of season; reprove, rebuke, exhort with all longsuffering and teaching" (2 Timothy 4:2).

Giving to God

At Bethel, too, Jacob made his vow, and covenanted his tithe. Of all he received, he would from now on give the tenth unto God. Again, the principle is clear. Bethel - the house of God - is the place in which the people of God can exercise the privilege of giving to Him. We need not trace the history of Israel to recognize the outworking of this principle. The Law made clear demands, and, in coming to God's house, the godly Israelite brought both sacrifices and freewill offerings. Still the privilege of giving to the Lord is part of the heritage of God's house. In our collective service on the first day of the week, as a holy priesthood we "offer up spiritual sacrifices, acceptable to God through Jesus Christ" (1 Peter 2:5). In addition, out of hearts which have themselves been yielded, God's people are able to give to Him of their possessions for the furtherance of the work of His house. The saints in Philippi were particularly commended for their exercise in this matter. Paul described their giving as "an odour of a sweet smell, a sacrifice acceptable, well-pleasing to God" (Philippians 4:18).

A holy place

Years had passed, Jacob had journeyed on from Bethel, and his twenty years of service to Laban lay behind. Once more, the word of the LORD came to him, "Arise, go up to Bethel, and dwell there" (Genesis 35:1). Here was a clear commandment. In preparing to obey, Jacob was aware of matters within his household which were inconsistent with Bethel. Strange gods were among them; these must be put away and they must purify themselves. "Holiness becometh thine house, O LORD, for evermore" (Psalm 93:5), was a principle applicable then as now. The Lord demands a high standard of spiritual integrity of those in His house. We should constantly search ourselves to ensure that we do not defile it.

On his return to Bethel God once more appeared to Jacob, repeating to him the glorious promises concerning his seed and the land. Little wonder that he once more set up a pillar of stone, on which he poured out a drink offering and poured oil thereon. Yet, once again we read that Jacob "journeyed from Bethel" (Genesis 35:16). One wonders why. Certainly, this departure from Bethel was marked by deep sorrow. For it was as they travelled, his beloved Rachel died. Yet again, "Israel journeyed, and spread his tent beyond the tower of Eder" (Genesis 35:21). Here again, Jacob faced grief, as his eldest son Reuben lay with Bilhah, his father's concubine - a sin which cost Reuben his birthright and his dying father's blessing.

How different things might have been had Jacob dwelt in Bethel, as the Lord had commanded him. For, to those who dwell there with a pure heart, the house of God is a place of blessing, "Blessed are they that dwell in Thy house: they will be still praising Thee" (Psalm 84:4). May it be ours to share in the desire expressed by Jacob's noble descendant, David, who, through all his days had a deep love for the house of God. "One thing have I asked of the LORD, that will I seek after; that I may dwell in the house of the LORD all the days of my life, to behold the beauty of the LORD, and to inquire in His temple" (Psalm 27:4).

10

CHAPTER TEN: JOSEPH AND HIS BROTHERS (JIM JOHNSTON)

There are some men who tower above their fellows in spiritual and moral stature - Joseph was such a man. Jacob, who had a God-given insight into the characters of his sons, described Joseph as one who was separate from his brethren (Genesis 49:26). In his youthful days he was grieved by their conduct and he brought an evil report of them to his father. There was a close affinity between Joseph and his father, and they enjoyed sweet fellowship together in Hebron, the place of fellowship. He became the object of his brothers' hatred because he was the special object of his father's love, and marked out as such by the coat he wore. Jacob may have been disposed to favour Joseph because he saw in him a strong likeness to the woman whose beauty had captivated him at first sight (Genesis 29:17; 39:6).

Joseph, however, was not only attractive in appearance, he displayed a beauty of character also; he was a worthy object for his father's love. Early in his life he learned to fear God and to depart from evil; these two things are complementary. The fear of God is a powerful restraining influence. It keeps from many a sin - it kept Joseph not only when he was in Hebron but also when he was in Egypt and subjected to many temptations.

In his youthful days in Hebron Joseph received, by means of his God-given dreams, some indication of the greatness that would one day be his. The telling of these dreams to his brothers, however, only served to increase their hatred of him. One day his father sent him out of the vale of Hebron to visit his brothers. He never returned to Hebron from that mission, and twenty-two eventful years ran their course before he saw his father again. Joseph is a type of the Lord Jesus as the sent One. He went out willingly to visit his brothers. He did not know what the future held for him, he only knew that he could expect little kindness from them, but still he went.

The Lord Jesus knew exactly the pathway He would tread when He came to earth, every detail of the agonizing experiences of Gethsemane, Gabbatha and Golgotha were known to Him before He came, yet He came willingly to do His Father's will, knowing it was to triumph at His cost.

Joseph arrived at Shechem and found that his brothers had left that place, but he did not turn back, he went on to Dothan and found them there. Like the One he typifies he was prepared to go the second mile. The hatred of his brothers was unmasked when he appeared. They were even prepared to kill him; Reuben's weak intervention prevented this in the first instance, then, indifferent to his tears and his pleadings, they sold him into slavery. Not only were they ruthless in dealing with Joseph; they were also heartless in their deception of their father, and hypocritical in seeking to comfort him (Genesis 37:35).

Joseph's brothers were responsible for their actions. They acted with evil intent, but in His overruling sovereignty God was working out His purposes. It is God's prerogative to bring good out of evil. Calvary is the supreme example of the wonderful way in which He does this. In such events we see divine sovereignty and human responsibility in simultaneous operation (Genesis 50:20; Acts 2:23).

Joseph was thus brought down to Egypt to become a lowly slave in a foreign land. Although alone in Egypt he was not completely forsaken, for God was with him. It is comforting to know that we cannot drift beyond God's love and care (Hebrews 13:5). Who can assess the solace that the consciousness of the divine presence brought to Joseph in that difficult phase of his life? The late teens are years of difficulty and conflict in most lives and they can be especially difficult if the young person is removed from the home influence and subjected to many pressures in a strange environment. Such considerations are pertinent to present-day conditions when young people frequently leave home at this period in their lives to find employment or to pursue a course of study at college or university.

It was the effect of his early training that gave Joseph the stability to resist the influences of the things around him. This once again underlines the value of early training. There were many lessons to be learned during this period of trial, but the fear of God kept him from falling a victim to temptation, and the consciousness of the divine presence sustained him. We do not take time to follow his promotion in Potiphar's house and the valuable administrative experience he gained there. God was preparing him for the high office he was destined to fill. God never thrusts great responsibility upon untried men. This principle holds good today in service in the house of God. There are qualities that can only be produced by adversity. This is borne out in the lives of all God's great men. They all felt the heat of the crucible in which they were proved in order to emerge approved for service.

Joseph might have been reasonably content with the place he had in Potiphar's house, but God had greater things in store for him. It was only the training ground for higher service, but first he had to know further trial and suffering before he reached the acme of his glory. Suffering, then glory was the pathway for Joseph and for his great Antitype (1 Peter 1:11). Perhaps there were times when he felt that all things were against him, but in retrospect he saw the perfection of the divine plan. The Lord chastens those whom He loves, but it is important to have the right attitude when we feel the pressure of God's hand upon us; then will the outcome be to our profit (Hebrews 12:6-11). Bitter experiences can be the gateway to blessing, and may open up avenues of greater usefulness in the service of God.

Joseph's promotion to the place of rule in Egypt was dramatically sudden but he was ready for it. Absolute authority was virtually his but having suffered so much himself through injustice we can be sure that he would use his authority wisely (Psalm 105: 21-22). It has been said that "Power tends to corrupt, and absolute power corrupts absolutely". If complete authority is placed in the hands of one man that man must be fitted to rule. In this, too, Joseph foreshadows Christ. We rejoice that ultimate authority in the universe is in the hands of the Man of Calvary. It could not be in better hands. Joseph was one of the greatest administrators this world has seen. He not only handled the famine crisis with consummate skill, meeting the need of a hungry world, but he also dealt with the emergency in such a way that a new relationship was established between Pharaoh and his subjects. In this also he prefigures Christ.

We pause to note that before Joseph was able to take up dealings with his brothers again we find him exalted, given a new name, and married to a Gentile bride - foreshadowings for the present time.

The revelation given to Joseph through the dreams of Pharaoh gave him an insight into the pattern of things for the future: seven years of plenty, followed by seven years of famine. He could also, perhaps, see a fulfilment of his dreams through his brothers coming down to Egypt for food, and bowing down to him, unaware of who he really was. How would he treat them if they came? It was not according to his nature to reward evil with evil, but he also understood the divine principle that repentance is a necessary pre-requisite for forgiveness. Joseph's dealings with his brothers, therefore, had the objective of bringing them to repentance. The retention of Simeon at his brothers' first visit, and his incrimination of Benjamin at their second visit, were all part of a plan to secure this objective. The powerful pleading of Judah touched Joseph deeply. It was a tremendous change from the callous indifference he displayed when Joseph had been sold into slavery.

Probably Judah had been the prime instigator then, now he was the prime pleader who was offering himself as a hostage to assuage his father's grief. A dramatic climax had been reached, the tender-hearted Joseph could restrain himself no longer, the time to make himself known had come. Joseph's brothers received the revelation with mixed feelings; they were troubled by his presence.

The revelation of Joseph to his brothers prefigures in a wonderful way the future dramatic revelation that will be made to Israel. Great will be their sorrow when they discover that the once despised Man of Calvary is their long-promised Messiah (Zechariah 12:10-14). The words of Isaiah 53 will then fittingly express their feelings in that day of national mourning.

The migration of Jacob and his family to Egypt, although ostensibly for the purpose of placing them where Joseph could readily provide for their needs, was in accordance with the divine purpose revealed to Abraham in Genesis 15:13-15. In the land of Goshen, under Joseph's care and protection, Jacob found peace and serenity in the last 17 years of his turbulent life, and Joseph's brothers found employment suitable for them and also beneficial to the state.

Troubled consciences are not easily stilled, and after Jacob's death Joseph's brothers sought an audience with him. They were afraid that Joseph's attitude to them might change. It was unworthy of them to entertain such thoughts. Their anxiety reveals how little they appreciated the nobility of their brother's character. In a greater and more wonderful way the One Joseph typifies is unchanging and unchangeable in His goodness (Hebrews 13:8).

The high-water mark of Joseph's faith was reached at the end of his life for the Holy Spirit selects the closing scene of his life to illustrate his faith (Hebrews 11:22). The glory of Egypt had not dimmed his spiritual vision nor diminished his faith. The promises of God meant more to the aged Joseph than the treasures of Egypt. He did not wish his body to be laid in the tombs of the Pharaohs amid the scenes of his earthly glory. He wanted rather to identify himself with the purpose of God concerning Israel (Genesis 50:25; Hebrews 11:22). Like his father he died in faith. The full realization of Joseph's longings and desires is yet future. He shall yet see a greater glory than Egypt, and experience the joyous fulfilment of those promises so precious to him (Hebrews 11).

We need to be vigilant lest the little material prosperity we may enjoy saps our spiritual vigour. Let us therefore, like Joseph, lay hold on the promises of God and have our vision filled with the eternal glories that are gleaming afar to nerve our faint endeavour.

CHAPTER ELEVEN: ISRAEL IN EGYPT (JOHN BAIRD)

God forewarned Abraham concerning Israel's time in Egypt, saying, "Know of a surety that thy seed shall be a stranger in a land that is not theirs, and shall serve them; and they shall afflict them four hundred years; and also that nation, whom they shall serve, will I judge: and afterward shall they come out with great substance" (Genesis 15:13,14).

That this prophecy was fulfilled in all respects is set forth in Stephen's address (Acts 7). The strange land was Egypt: the duration of the sojourn, the affliction there, and the final deliverance were all in strict accord with the word to Abraham (Exodus 1-14). It is remarkable that the Lord, while giving to Abraham the assurance of notable promises regarding the land, the numerous seed and the Seed (in whom all nations of the earth should be blessed), at the same time foretold the distress of Israel in Egypt. God never acts on the basis of an afterthought: He knows the end from the beginning (Isaiah 46:10).

The manner of fulfilment is characteristic of the works of God, who sent Joseph into Egypt in advance of his father and his brothers. In their envy and hatred his brothers sold him to passing merchants who sold him into Egypt (Genesis 37:28,36; 39:1). There Joseph, falsely accused, suffered imprisonment for a time, but the Lord ordered events so that at thirty years of age he was exalted by Pharaoh to be his grand vizier (Genesis 39-46). His great work there was not the saving of the people of Egypt from disastrous famine but rather the preserving alive of the chosen race, for God had sent him before them (Psalm 105:17). We pause here to observe that there are often two sides to the things that befall us, the human side (usually the more apparent) and the divine side (which usually requires to be revealed by God).

In Joseph's case the human side consisted in his brethren's action in selling him into Egypt, an action based on unbrotherly jealousy. The divine side is seen in God's provision of a man "to save much people alive" (Genesis 50:20), including all of the chosen people, an action arising from divine love and foreknowl-edge. In the course of time both sides became apparent to Joseph, who sought to comfort his repentant brothers by revealing the truth to them (Genesis 45:5). We in our day have cause to be thankful for the record of the happenings to Joseph, for they show him as a notably complete type of Christ, who was sent into the world to bring life eternal to us.

Having at last revealed his identity to his brothers, Joseph sent them back to their father not only with the much needed corn but also with all that was necessary to enable the aged Jacob to journey from Canaan to Egypt, and 'to bring with him all the souls of his house (Genesis 46:27). Joseph left nothing undone that was necessary to ensure reunion with his father; likewise our Saviour is our assurance of being with Him in the eternal day.

In the course of the journey to Egypt Jacob offered sacrifices at Beersheba, and there God revealed to him that the going down into Egypt was in accordance with His purposes, and gave him the reassuring word, "I will go down with thee into Egypt; and I will also surely bring thee up again: and Joseph shall put his hand upon thine eyes" (Genesis 46:4). Jacob therefore went down into Egypt assured that God was with him, and, though he would die there, the nation would be brought back to the land that God had promised to him and to Abraham and Isaac before him.

Joseph purposed to place his father and his brothers in Goshen (Genesis 46:34) and Pharaoh readily consented (Genesis 47:6). Goshen, where the best pastures were located, was chosen because Jacob and his sons were "keepers of cattle" and the Egyptians abominated shepherds (Genesis 46:34). By this means Joseph kept his promise to his brothers that they should have "the good of the land" (Genesis 45:18,20). This provision along with the generous welcome extended by Pharaoh to Jacob would seem contrary to the circumstance that the Egyptians abominated shepherds. To resolve this apparent paradox some point out that the Pharaoh of the time of Joseph was one of the Hyksos Pharaohs. These Hyksos were Semitic in origin and pastoral in interests and occupation, and so the Hyksos (who then dominated Egypt) were themselves hated by the indigenous Egyptians.

If this be the true explanation, we can see divine pre-vision and provision in the advent of the Hyksos, for, if an indigenous Egyptian had occupied the throne, it is most unlikely that Jacob and his company would have been so well treated. If this be a sound elucidation of the paradox, it may shed light on other matters. The favour shown to Jacob and his house continued until at least beyond the death of Joseph, hence the children of Israel were not under taskmasters during the entire sojourn in Egypt. On the other hand, the affliction was fully established before the birth of Moses, who was eighty years of age when he returned to lead the people out. In the Scriptures and in secular history there is no definite indication of the time when Israel began to be afflicted, and there are those who use this circumstance as an excuse for unbelief. Scripture is not alone in saying but little about the main period of the time in Egypt.

Egyptian records are notably meagre in this very period. Beginning with the coming to power of the Hyksos and extending through approximately the next four hundred years, Egyptian records are very sparse in comparison with those before and after that period. But, if the Hyksos themselves were hated by the indigenous Egyptians, this may explain why the Egyptian scribes might withhold information from posterity. (Or it may well be that the relevant records are still undiscovered.) For our part, we accept by faith the record in Genesis and Exodus as inspired Scripture.

A considerable amount of detail is given in Genesis as to the going down into Egypt and in Exodus as to the going out, but of the main period of the time in Egypt we have little in the way of detail. There is an informative account of the death of Jacob and of his burial. In blessing his sons before he died (Genesis 49) Jacob spoke of the things which should befall them in the latter days, and it would appear that the future was to reflect the past. Reuben, the firstborn, did not inherit the promise of the Messiah: a sinful act unfitted him. This valued promise went to Judah. Again, the scattering of Levi in Israel was predicted. Also, Joseph is still presented as a type of Christ. Jacob indeed looked forward to more than the settlement in the land: he prophesied concerning the promised Seed, Christ.

Having blessed his sons, Jacob charged them that they should bury him in the cave in the field of Ephron the Hittite, the burying place purchased by Abraham. As they journeyed to Canaan to do so, they were accompanied by all the servants of Pharaoh, the elders of his house, and all the elders of the land of Egypt (Genesis 50:7). This is not consistent with enslavement and rigorous bondage, but rather indicates sympathetic and favourable treatment from Pharaoh up to and beyond the death of Jacob.

Similar circumstances appear to have prevailed until after the death of Joseph, who also died in Egypt, for there is no word as to affliction prior to it. The affliction of Israel began at a later date when the children of Israel had greatly multiplied and in the time of a Pharaoh who did not know Joseph, probably a Pharaoh of another dynasty who refused to recognize Egypt's indebtedness to Joseph (Exodus 1:7,8; Acts 7:17,18). Pharaoh was like many unregenerate ones today: they refuse to acknowledge the saving work of Christ and also fail to recognize God's bountiful provision for their temporal needs.

Jacob and Joseph both desired to be buried in the cave with Abraham and Isaac because, while they were experiencing God's blessing in Egypt, their hearts were in Canaan: such was their estimate of the promises of God. It is commonly accepted that as to our Christian experience the world is typified by Egypt: it is not our home. While we must live here, enjoying the blessing of God and testifying to His saving grace, our inmost desires for ourselves are centred on the eternal state: "looking for and earnestly desiring the coming of the day of God" (2 Peter 3:12). It behoves us therefore not to be overmuch taken up with the things of this life, but rather to fulfil our period of service in the light of the eternal day.

The Genesis record takes us up to the death of Joseph, and as a consequence the circumstances attending the going out are relevant to a study of Exodus, the early chapters of which indicate the conditions that prevailed in Egypt in the days of the enforced labour and bondage. The children of Israel were made to build store cities for Pharaoh, Pithom and Raamses (Exodus 1:11). The forced labour would not be pleasant, but through it they would gather knowledge and skill in building, which would prove an asset when they were settling in Canaan, and possibly also in the making of the tabernacle in the wilderness. Experience in building cities was necessary, for, since the call of Abraham, his progeny were tent-dwellers, at least up to the going down into Egypt.

But not all that they acquired in Egypt was safe and good. They had learned a taste for the foods of Egypt (Numbers 11:5), and in the wilderness they despised the God-given manna and lusted after the pleasant things of Egypt. While we are in the world, we cannot but gather many things from the world, things possibly good and bad: but in our days of service Godward we should be careful as to the effect these may have on our thoughts and ways. It is good to see a man highly competent in the skills he has acquired, especially if he makes it his aim to consecrate the good skills in service for God: the other things, the bad and the dubious, he should reject and seek to be fully nourished in the things of God.

12

CHAPTER TWELVE: CONCLUSION (LAURIE BURROWS)

Concluding our studies in the book of Genesis we wish first of all to return to our introductory theme that, with the rest of the Bible, this ancient book was written for man's spiritual instruction, being divinely inspired, and that its account of origins is authentic and accurate. We are aware that there are many today who would not agree with such an assessment. "Hath God said?" was the subtle introduction to Satan's first temptation; it is still one of his most effective approaches. His attempt to undermine confidence in God's word is especially directed against its first book because, as this book shows, it is the basis upon which the rest of the Bible is built.

If Genesis is removed the remainder loses its cohesion, the doctrine of the gospel becomes meaningless, the beginnings of matter and life, the origin of sin and man's relationship with his Creator are all placed at the mercy of philosophical speculation. So the adversary, in promoting doubt and unbelief about the Genesis account of the beginning of things, gains his objective of destroying faith in the Bible and the God of the Bible. Without God to obey and divine revelation to guide him man loses all sense of direction. He follows his own natural desires, regardless of the claims of his Creator. The results are seen in the degradation which pervades the world today.

So widespread and persistent is the general rejection of the Biblical account of creation that even believers are being affected by it, some perhaps only subconsciously, but nevertheless with the effect that the word of God tends to have less authority in their hearts than it once had. Others feel the need to seek some sort of compromise so as to avoid being classed as cranks for not accepting the conclusions of modern science. One such compromise is based on the idea that much of Genesis is purely figurative. Examination of what contributors have written in this book shows that none has for a moment entertained such a suggestion. In fact, God's dealings with men as individuals has frequently been emphasized, thus testifying to the literalness of the record. In our first chapter issue the falsity of legendary interpretations was demonstrated, and similar arguments may be used in reply to figurative theories of the Genesis account of man's creation.

There is plenty of other scriptural evidence on the subject but we just mention one point for further thought. In Luke 3:23-38 Jesus is mentioned in the same genealogy as Jacob, Isaac, Abraham, Noah, Methuselah, Seth, Adam and many other Old Testament worthies. The humanity and personality of the Lord Jesus authenticates the same in relation to Adam and the patriarchs.

Another way of avoiding a direct confrontation between Genesis and modern philosophy is to allege that there are serious difficulties in interpreting the story of creation, but in due course, when further light has been obtained, evolutionary theories will be seen to be in accord with the Biblical account. If the Bible is God's revelation to man, it must be capable of being understood, at least in its essentials, by ordinary people.

We have seen that Genesis is a necessary part of this revelation and that it is vital that man should have a correct understanding of his relationship with his Creator. Is it therefore conceivable that an all-wise God would allow such important teaching to be shrouded in mystery or be dependent upon modern scholarship for its interpretation? If scientific theories seem to contradict the plain word of Scripture, it is surely proper for the Christian to question the validity of those theories before suggesting that the Bible needs re-interpretation. The book of Genesis will not yield its meaning to human genius, it must be studied in the same way as the rest of God's word: by comparing scripture with scripture under the guidance of the Holy Spirit, a method as profitable for the unlearned as for the scholar. As in all spiritual things it is not merely a matter of intellect but of faith, for "by faith we understand that the worlds have been framed by the word of God" (Hebrews 11:3).

During the book, attention has been drawn to God's early dealings with men, including the creation of Adam and Eve, their eviction from the garden of Eden, the Flood, the scattering from Babel, the call of Abraham, and the various ways in which Isaac, Jacob and Joseph experienced divine protection and over-ruling in their lives. Sometimes God's might was displayed and sometimes less spectacular means were used, but always there can be seen the heavenly purposes of grace to men which were to find their fuller manifestation in the coming of the Christ.

Following the disobedience of Adam and Eve, the story of Genesis is largely one of sin and death. Even in those early days men "exchanged the truth of God for a lie and worshipped and served the creature rather than the Creator" (Romans 1:25), so that no deed was too evil for them to perpetrate. The terrible results of the error of our first parents soon became obvious, filling the earth with violence (Genesis 6:11) and demanding the judgement of God. This took the form of a Flood the like of which had never been seen before nor ever will be again. "All the high mountains that were under the whole heaven were covered", and except for Noah and his family "every living thing was destroyed which was upon the face of the ground" (Genesis 7;19,23); hard for us to envisage but presenting no difficulty to the omnipotent Creator. Words of similar import to those already quoted occur no less than twelve times in the Genesis account, in strong confirmation of a world-wide inundation.

It is truly surprising how quickly divine visitation is forgotten. Soon after the greatest catastrophe ever to come upon men they were joining forces to oppose God and manage their affairs without Him. Their schemes were nipped in the bud when their language was confounded at Babel, but man's dream of absolute supremacy in defiance of God has been pursued down the ages. In later days Nebuchadnezzar was its great exponent, until he was taught that God rules in the kingdom of men (Daniel 4:25,32). In the last days a man will aspire to supremacy in heaven as well as on earth, his capital will also be Babylon, but complete and final destruction will suddenly overtake both him and his city (Revelation 18:21-24; 19:19-21).

As the story of Genesis unfolds little is said about the generality of men, but divine choice lays hold on a certain man of the godly line of Shem named Abraham with whom God deals in a very intimate way. This man and his descendants, Isaac and Jacob, lived in tents in a strange land and although at times straying from their divinely appointed path, they nevertheless enjoyed times of close communion with God, who promised them a country of their own and assured them of a glorious national future. Moreover, as stated in chapter six, "the great end in view in all this was Christ. Christ the Seed of Abraham (Galatians 3:16); the One through whom all things would be reconciled to God (Colossians 1:20); who came to take away the sin of the world (John 1:29); the Person in whom all things in heaven and upon the earth would be summed up (Ephesians 1:10)".

One aim of this book has been to bring before readers some references in Genesis to the scriptural teaching about man's sinful nature, his need of salvation and God's provision for him in the perfect sacrifice of Christ, not only to ensure eternal life as a free gift to be received by faith, but also to enable the believer to cleanse his ways and serve God on earth. Abraham's tent in the wilderness is a symbol of the holy life God expects to see in the believer, and his altar a symbol of the divine service and worship to be engaged in when, Jacob-like, the believer comes by God's grace to the place where He dwells; "this is none other but the house of God, and this is the gate of heaven" (Genesis 28:17).

ABOUT THE PUBLISHER

Hayes Press (www.hayespress.org) is a registered charity in the United Kingdom, whose primary mission is to disseminate the Word of God, mainly through literature. It is one of the largest distributors of gospel tracts and leaflets in the United Kingdom, with over 100 titles and many thousands dispatched annually. In addition to paperbacks and eBooks, Hayes Press also publishes Plus Eagles' Wings, a fun and educational Bible magazine for children, and Golden Bells, a popular daily Bible reading calendar in wall or desk formats.

If you would like to contact Hayes Press, there are a number of ways you can do so:

By mail: c/o The Barn, Flaxlands, Royal Wootton Bassett, Wiltshire, UK SN4 8DY

By phone: 01793 850598

By eMail: info@hayespress.org

via Facebook: www.facebook.com/hayespress.org